LIGHTNING BOLT BOOKS™

T0033522

Look Inside a Bulldozer

How It Works

Brianna Kaiser

Lerner Publications • Minneapolis

Lerner Publications Company
An imprint of Lerner Publishing Group, Inc.
241 First Avenue North
Minneapolis, MN 55401 USA

For reading levels and more information, look up this title at www.lernerbooks.com.

Main body text set in Billy Infant Regular. Typeface provided by SparkType.

Editor: Annie Zheng **Designer:** Martha Kranes **Photo Editor:** Nicole Berglund
Lerner team: Sue Marquis

Library of Congress Cataloging-in-Publication Data

Names: Kaiser, Brianna, 1996- author.
Title: Look inside a bulldozer : how it works / Brianna Kaiser.
Description: Minneapolis : Lerner Publications, [2024] | Series: Lightning bolt books. Under the hood | Includes bibliographical references and index. | Audience: Ages 6-9 | Audience: Grades 2-3 | Summary: "Bulldozers are powerful machines that dig and carry heavy loads. But that's not all they do! Readers will love learning about different types of bulldozers, how they're used, and more in this fun book"— Provided by publisher.
Identifiers: LCCN 2023013911 (print) | LCCN 2023013912 (ebook) | ISBN 9798765608340 (lib. bdg.) | ISBN 9798765624364 (pbk.) | ISBN 9798765615621 (epub)
Subjects: LCSH: Bulldozers—Juvenile literature. | Earthwork—Juvenile literature. | BISAC: JUVENILE NONFICTION / Transportation / General
Classification: LCC TA735 .K35 2024 (print) | LCC TA735 (ebook) | DDC 629.225—dc23/ eng/20230329

LC record available at https://lccn.loc.gov/2023013911
LC ebook record available at https://lccn.loc.gov/2023013912

Manufactured in the United States of America
1-1009612-51488-6/6/2023

Table of Contents

What Are Bulldozers?

A person digs a hole using a powerful machine. Then the machine carries away all the dirt it dug up. But what is the person driving? It's a bulldozer!

People use bulldozers for many types of jobs. Bulldozers can dig up dirt or soil. They can also push or carry heavy objects.

People use the front part of bulldozers to move objects.

Many construction workers use bulldozers to get an area ready for building. They also use bulldozers to make the ground flat for a road.

Bulldozers clear away dirt on roads to make the ground smooth.

Farmers use bulldozers to clear large objects off their land. They use bulldozers to spread soil too. Then the farmers can grow foods and plants.

A bulldozer near a barn

Types and uses

There are three main types of bulldozers. Crawler bulldozers are good for moving heavy objects. They are also called track bulldozers.

Wheel bulldozers are the biggest type. They are the best for working on soft ground. They are often used to make the ground flat.

Wheel bulldozers are also called tire bulldozers.

Mini bulldozers are the smallest kind. They are good for jobs in smaller spaces. They're often used for driveways or roadsides.

Mini bulldozers can be used to clear rocks, shrubs, or tree stumps in front of houses.

Blades are made of metal and come in different shapes and sizes.

Bulldozers have a blade on the front. The blade is the part that digs or moves objects.

How Bulldozers Work

Cabs are where a person sits. Cabs have buttons and joysticks. These control how the bulldozer moves.

To drive the bulldozer, the person moves the driving joystick forward or backward. To stop, the person presses their foot down on the brake pedal.

The left joystick is for driving. The right joystick is to move the blade.

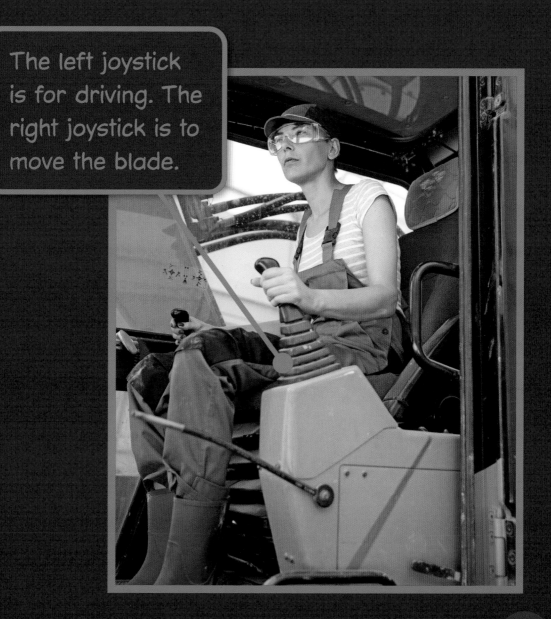

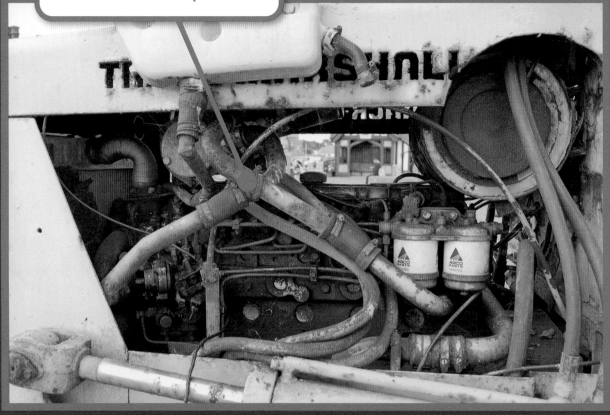

Engines make bulldozers work.
Bulldozer engines run by
turning diesel, a type of fuel,
into energy.

Bulldozers with tracks are better for hard or uneven ground. Bulldozers with tires are better for softer ground.

Bulldozer tracks

Cool Parts

Different parts can be added to bulldozers. Rippers are put on the back of bulldozers. They help break up hard ground.

Rakes remove trees, rocks, or other big objects that have fallen. They are put on the front of a bulldozer.

Using rakes to move objects is helpful because it doesn't disturb the soil.

Winches are cables or ropes. They are put on the back of a bulldozer. They can be used to move heavy objects or clear paths.

Winches are often used to pull and move fallen trees.

People all around the world use bulldozers.

Bulldozers are used for many jobs. What would you use them for? What kind of bulldozer would you use?

Bulldozer Diagram

cab

track

blade

Tracks

A bulldozer's track should not be too tight or too loose. If a track is too loose, it could fall off. It can also make the bulldozer bounce more. That makes it harder for the bulldozer to make the ground level. If a track is too tight, it gets worn down faster. A bulldozer needs a new track if the old one is too worn down.

Glossary

blade: the part of a bulldozer that digs or moves objects

cab: the part of the bulldozer a person sits in to control the bulldozer

construction: the act of building something

energy: the power to make something work

rake: a part of a bulldozer that removes objects

ripper: a part of a bulldozer that breaks up ground

track: the part some bulldozers use to move

winch: a cable or rope on a bulldozer used to move objects

Learn More

Britannica Kids: Bulldozer
https://kids.britannica.com/students/article/bulldozer/273398

Jaske, Julia. *Look, a Bulldozer!* Ann Arbor, MI: Cherry Lake, 2022.

Kiddle: Bulldozer Facts for Kids
https://kids.kiddle.co/Bulldozer

Leed, Percy. *Look Inside a Big Rig: How It Works*. Minneapolis: Lerner Publications, 2024.

Loy, Harriet. *A Bulldozer's Day*. Minneapolis: Bellwether Media, Inc., 2023.

Index

Photo Acknowledgments

Image credits: Avalon_Studio/Getty Images, p. 4; LETOPISEC/Shutterstock, p. 5; fotog/Getty Images, p. 6; happycreator/Shutterstock, p. 7; kozmoat98/Getty Images, p. 8; ewg3D/Getty Images, p. 9; ungvar/Shutterstock, p. 10; Roberto/Getty Images, p. 11; Jeffrey Isaac Greenberg 12+/Alamy, p. 12; CasarsaGuru/Getty Images, p. 13; David Ludlow/Alamy, p. 14; Chris Jongkind/Getty Images, p. 15; Juan Enrique del Barrio/Shutterstock, p. 16; Wesley Otero/Shutterstock, p. 17; kellyvandellen/Getty Images, p. 18; master_77/Shutterstock, p. 19; Vereshchagin Dmitry/Shutterstock, p. 20.

Cover: Valentin Valkov/Shutterstock.